CHANUKAH TODAY
THE NEW HOLIDAY SONGBOOK

Project Manager
Michael Boxer

Editors
Rachel Wetstein
Joshua Wiczer

TRANSCONTINENTAL
MUSIC Publications
The world's leading publisher of Jewish music since 1938

CHANUKAH TODAY

© 2012 Transcontinental Music Publications
CD © 2012 Transcontinental Music Publications
633 Third Avenue - New York, NY 10017 - Fax 212.650.4119
212.650.4105 - **TranscontinentalMusic.com** - tmp@urj.org
A division of URJ Books and Music
URJBooksAndMusic.com

Printed in the United States of America
Cover design by Michael Silber
Book design by Joshua Wiczer
CD produced by Michael Boxer
ISBN 978-0-8074-1238-1 - Item no. 993468
10 9 8 7 6 5 4 3 2 1

More resources for Chanukah and other Jewish holidays may be found at
TranscontinentalMusic.com
URJBooksAndMusic.com
URJ.org

PROJECT COMMITTEE

Michael Boxer

Steve Brodsky

Alan Goodis

Danielle Rodnizki

Hebrew Pronunciation Guide

VOWELS

a as in *father*

ai as in *aisle* (= long *i* as in *ice*)

e = short *e* as in *bed*

ei as in *eight* (= long *a* as in *ace*)

i as in *pizza* (= long *e* as in *be*)

o = long *o* as in *go*

u = long *u* as in *lunar*

' = unstressed vowel close to ə or unstressed short *e*

oi as in *boy*

CONSONANTS

ch as in German *Bach* or Scottish *loch* (not as in *cheese*)

g = hard *g* as in *get* (not soft *g* as in *gem*)

tz = as in *boats*

h after a vowel is silent

CHANUKAH TODAY

CHANUKAH TODAY

THE NEW HOLIDAY SONGBOOK

TO BE A LIGHT BY DAN NICHOLS AND E18HTEEN

MUSIC & TEXT: DAN NICHOLS

it's not just an ech - o___ that we let___ go___ and___ for-get

'cause no-thing burns deep - er___ than___ the___ fi - res___ of___ re-gret___

no - thing burns deep - er___ than___ the___ fi - res___ of___ re-gret___

there's no to - mor - row.___

OCHO KANDELIKAS BY DELEON

MUSIC AND TEXT: FLORY JAGODA

CD TRACK ②

993468

Arrangement © 2008 Golemite (ASCAP)

mi, o - cho kan - de - las pa - ra mi, o - cho kan - de - las pa - ra

mi,_____ o - cho kan - de - las pa - ra mi._____

1. Beautiful Hanukah is here,
eight candles for me.

One candle, two candles,
three candles, four candles,
five candles, six candles,
seven candles, eight candles for me.

2. There will be a lot of parties,
with joy and happiness.

1. Hanukah linda sta aki,
ocho kandelas para mi.

Una kandelika, dos kandelikas,
tres kandelikas, kuatro kandelikas,
sintyu kandeikas, sej kandelikas,
siete kandelikas, ocho kandelas para mi.

2. Muchas fiestas vo fazer,
con alegrias i plazer.

CHANUKAH BLESSINGS BY THE BARENAKED LADIES

MUSIC & TEXT: STEPHEN PAGE

CD TRACK ③

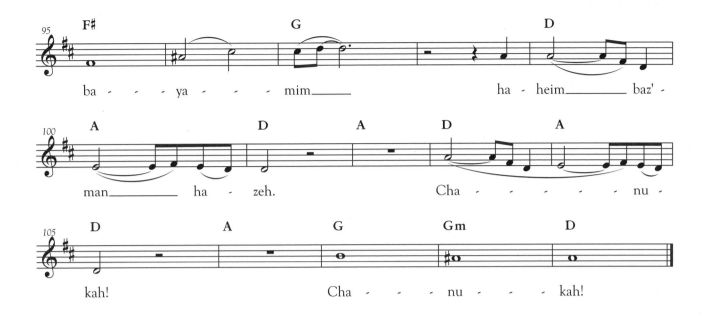

Blessed are You, Adonai our God,
Sovereign of all,
who hallows us with mitzvot,
commanding us to kindle the Chanukah lights.

Blessed are You, Adonai our God,
Sovereign of all,
who performed wondrous deeds for our ancestors
in days of old at this season.

בָּרוּךְ אַתָּה, יְיָ אֱלֹהֵינוּ,
מֶלֶךְ הָעוֹלָם,
אֲשֶׁר קִדְּשָׁנוּ בְּמִצְוֹתָיו
וְצִוָּנוּ לְהַדְלִיק נֵר שֶׁל חֲנֻכָּה.

בָּרוּךְ אַתָּה, יְיָ אֱלֹהֵינוּ,
מֶלֶךְ הָעוֹלָם,
שֶׁעָשָׂה נִסִּים לַאֲבוֹתֵינוּ
בַּיָּמִים הָהֵם בַּזְּמַן הַזֶּה.

12

THE DREIDEL SONG BY JULIE SILVER

MUSIC & TEXT: JULIE SILVER

PASS THE CANDLE BY MICHELLE CITRIN

MUSIC & LYRICS : MICHELLE CITRIN AND WILLIAM LEVIN

CD TRACK 5

To - night we light_____ the Cha - nu - kah can - dles_ from

(left to_ right,_____ left to_ right,_____

left to_ right._ left to_ right,_____ left to_ right)_

Our

favo - rite time_ of year_ is here, the fes - ti - val of lights,_____ we

cel - e - brate_ our vic - to - ry, we ce - le - brate_ our right._ First you

take a sin - gle can - dle and you start it with a spark,_ then you

pass it all_ a - round_ the world, bring light un - to_ the dark._ To -

IN THESE LIGHTS BY JOSH NELSON

MUSIC & TEXT: JOSH NELSON

Medium Rock (♩ = 108)

1. In the days___ when we___ were bro-ken,___ in the nights___ when we___ were fall-ing fast,___ in the times ___ when hope___ was hard___ to find,___ the times when love___ was left___ ___ be-hind,___ You came to lead___ us home.___

In this sto-ry of___ re-demp - tion,___ in this tale___ that we___ will al-ways tell,___ in the leg- -end of___ our vic - to-ry,___ a he-ro came___ to set___ us free,___ to

993468

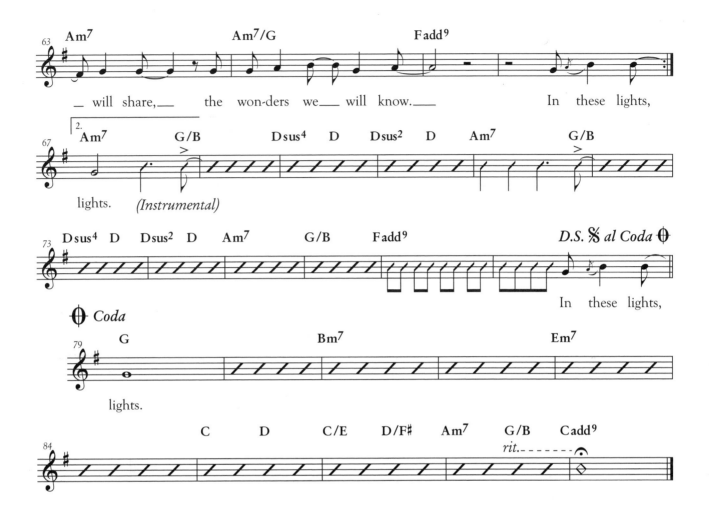

_ will share,___ the won-ders we__ will know.___ In these lights,

lights. *(Instrumental)*

D.S. 𝄋 al Coda 𝄌

In these lights,

𝄌 *Coda*

lights.

rit.- - - - - - -

AL HANISSIM BY CRAIG TAUBMAN

MUSIC: CRAIG TAUBMAN
TEXT: CHANUKAH LITURGY

על הנסים

CD TRACK (7)

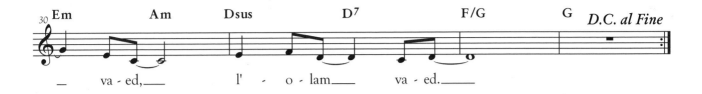

_ va - ed,___ l' - o - lam___ va - ed.___

We give thanks for the redeeming wonders
and he mighty deeds by which,
at this season,
our people was saved in days of old.

For all these things, O Sovereign,
let your Name be forever praised and blessed.

עַל הַנִּסִּים, וְעַל הַפֻּרְקָן,
וְעַל הַגְּבוּרוֹת, וְעַל הַתְּשׁוּעוֹת,
וְעַל הַמִּלְחָמוֹת, שֶׁעָשִׂיתָ לַאֲבוֹתֵינוּ
בַּיָּמִים הָהֵם, בַּזְּמַן הַזֶּה.

וְעַל כֻּלָּם יִתְבָּרַךְ וְיִתְרוֹמַם שִׁמְךָ
מַלְכֵּנוּ תָּמִיד לְעוֹלָם וָעֶד.

HANEIROT HALALU BY STACY BEYER

MUSIC: *STACY BEYER*
TEXT: *CHANUKAH LITURGY*

הנרות הללו

CD TRACK (8)

Rock (♩ = 132)

1. We light these lights for the mir-a-cles, for the won-der. We light these lights to re-joice and to re-mem-ber. We light these lights for the days of the sea-son. We light these lights as a sym-bol of our free-dom. Ha-nei-rot, ha-nei-rot, ha-la-lu.

ha-la-lu, ha-la-lu, ha-la-lu,

Ha-nei-rot, ha-nei-rot, ha-la-lu.

ha-la-lu, ha-la-lu, ha-la-lu,

* N.B.: On D.S., Instrumental/Solo until Chorus

993468

These candles do we light.
A great miracle happened there.

הַגֵּרוֹת הַלָּלוּ.
נֵס גָּדוֹל הָיָה שָׁם.

EIGHT NIGHTS OF JOY
BY RABBI JOE BLACK & THE MAXWELL STREET KLEZMER BAND

MUSIC & TEXT: RABBI JOE BLACK

CD TRACK 9

993468

one, two, three, four, five,___ six, se-ven, eight nights of joy,___ from the

streets of Tel A-viv___ to Chi-ca-go, Ill-in-ois. Cha-nu-kah is fun for moms and

dads and girls and boys. Yes it's one, two, three, four, five,___ six,

se-ven, eight nights of joy.___ 2. Eight___ small can-dles___

stand-ing in a row,___ put them in the win - dow___ so

all can see their glow.___ And though it's dark out - side___ our

faith it will___ a - bide re - mem - ber - ing those mir - a - cles___ that

hap-pened long a - go. Oh, one, two, three, four, five,___ six,

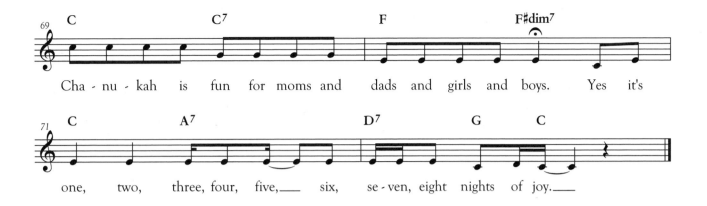

Cha - nu - kah is fun for moms and dads and girls and boys. Yes it's

one, two, three, four, five,___ six, se - ven, eight nights of joy.___

HOW DO YOU SPELL CHANNUKKAHH? BY THE LEEVEES

MUSIC & TEXT: ADAM GARDNER AND DAVE SCHNEIDER

CD TRACK 10

Copyright © 2005 Gyro Spit Music (ASCAP) / Jewshi Music (BMI)

THE CANDLES OF CHANUKAH BY SOULAVIV

MUSIC AND LYRICS: ROB RAEDE

CD TRACK 11

(Instrumental Introduction)

We light the can-dles of Cha - nu - kah,__ oh,__ Cha - nu - kah,__ oh__ oh.

Come see the can-dles of Cha - nu - kah,__ oh,__ Cha - nu - kah,__ oh__ oh.

We light the can-dles of Cha - nu - kah,__ oh,__ Cha - nu - kah,__ oh__ oh.

We light the can-dles of Cha - nu - kah,__ oh,__ Cha - nu - kah,__ oh__ oh.

Come see the can-dles of Cha - nu - kah,__ oh,__ Cha - nu - kah,__ oh__ oh.__

Come see the can-dles of Cha - nu - kah,__ oh,__ Cha - nu - kah,__ oh__ oh.__

Copyright © 2009 Robert Reade

(Guitar Interlude)

NIGHT BY NIGHT BY BETH SCHAFER

MUSIC & TEXT: BETH SCHAFER

CD TRACK 12

993468

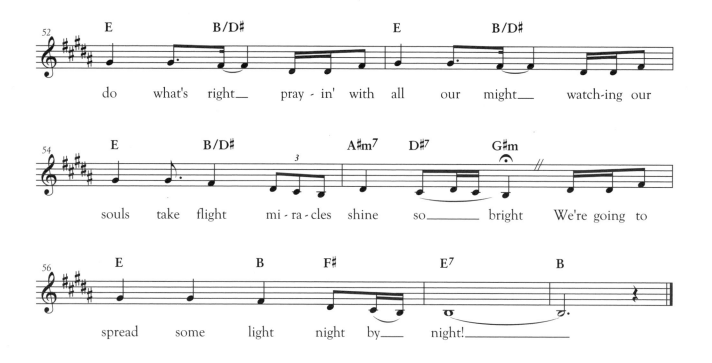

JAZZ OF AGES BY ERIC KOMAR

MUSIC: BASED ON ROCK OF AGES (TRADITIONAL)

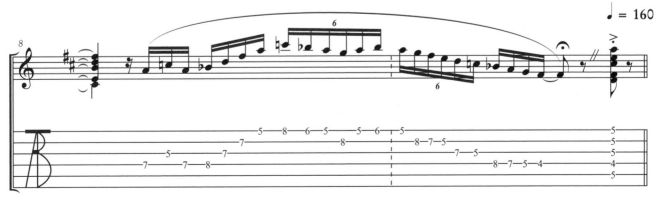

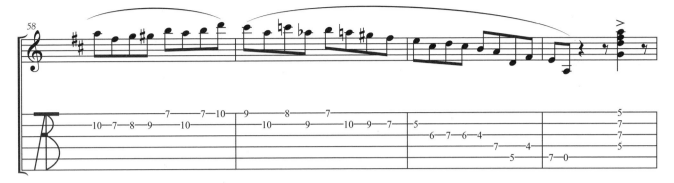

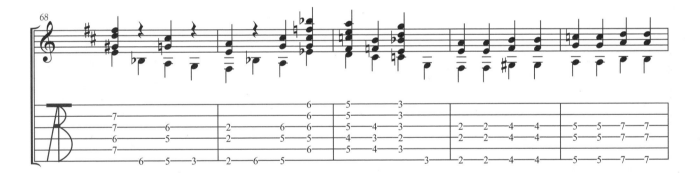

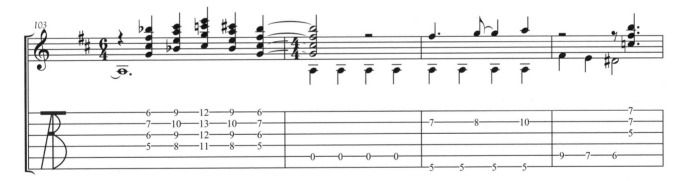

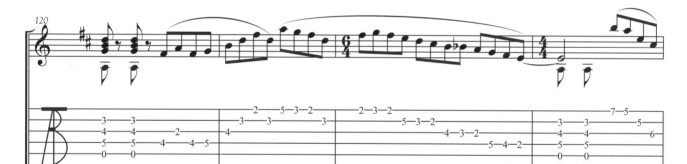

LIGHT THESE LIGHTS / CHANUKAH BLESSINGS BY DEBBIE FRIEDMAN

MUSIC & ENGLISH TEXT: *DEBBIE FRIEDMAN*
HEBREW TEXT: *CHANUKAH LITURGY*

CD TRACK 14

Copyright © 1995 Deborah Lynn Friedman (ASCAP)

Blessed are You, Adonai our God,
Sovereign of all,
who hallows us with mitzvot,
commanding us to kindle the Chanukah lights.

בָּרוּךְ אַתָּה, יְיָ אֱלֹהֵינוּ,
מֶלֶךְ הָעוֹלָם,
אֲשֶׁר קִדְּשָׁנוּ בְּמִצְוֹתָיו
וְצִוָּנוּ לְהַדְלִיק נֵר שֶׁל חֲנֻכָּה.

Blessed are You, Adonai our God,
Sovereign of all,
who performed wondrous deeds for our ancestors
in days of old at this season.

בָּרוּךְ אַתָּה, יְיָ אֱלֹהֵינוּ,
מֶלֶךְ הָעוֹלָם,
שֶׁעָשָׂה נִסִּים לַאֲבוֹתֵינוּ
בַּיָּמִים הָהֵם בַּזְּמַן הַזֶּה.

Blessed are You, Adonai our God,
Sovereign of all,
for giving us life, for sustaining us,
and for enabling us to reach this season.

בָּרוּךְ אַתָּה, יְיָ אֱלֹהֵינוּ
מֶלֶךְ הָעוֹלָם,
שֶׁהֶחֱיָנוּ וְקִיְּמָנוּ
וְהִגִּיעָנוּ לַזְּמַן הַזֶּה.

993468

The *Chanukah Today* CD accompanying this book is also available separately
(TMP item no. 950149)

Track information for accompanying CD

1. To Be A Light (D. Nichols)
Performed by Dan Nichols and E18hteen
© 2011 Dan Nichols
Previously unreleased

2. Ocho Kandelikas (F. Jagoda)
Performed by DeLeon
© 2008 Golemite
From the album *JDub Presents Jewltide*

3. Chanukah Blessings (S. Page)
Performed by Barenaked Ladies
© 2004 WB Music Corp. (ASCAP) and
    Fresh Baked Goods (NS). All rights
    administered by WB Music Corp.
From the album *Barenaked for the Holidays*

4. The Dreidel Song (J. Silver)
Performed by Julie Silver
© 2005 Julie A. Silver, A Silver Girl Music (ASCAP)
From the album *It's Chanukah Time*

5. Pass the Candle (From Left to Right)
(M. Citrin and W. Levin)
Performed by Michelle Citrin
© 2008 Honk If You Like Music (BMI)
    and William H. Levin (ASCAP)
As seen on YouTube and released as a single

6. In These Lights (J. Nelson)
Performed by Josh Nelson
© 2009 Josh Nelson Music BMI
From the forthcoming album *In These Lights*

7. Al Hanisim (C. Taubman)
Performed by Craig Taubman
© 1988 Sweet Louise Music
From the album *Best of the Rest*

8. Haneirot Halalu (S. Beyer)
Performed by Stacy Beyer
© 2005 SHAELI Songs (ASCAP)
From the album *Must Be Chanukah*

9. Eight Nights of Joy (J. Black)
Performed by Rabbi Joe Black
    and the Maxwell Street Klezmer Band
© 2006 Lanitunes Music
From the album *Eight Nights of Joy*

10. How Do You Spell Channukkahh?
(A. Gardner and D. Schneider)
Performed by The Leevees
© 2005 Gyro Spit Music (ASCAP) /
    Jewshi Music (BMI)
From the album *Hanukkah Rocks*

11. The Candles of Chanukah (R. Raede)
Performed by SoulAviv
© 2009 Robert Reade
Previously unreleased

12. Night by Night (B. Schafer)
Performed by Beth Schafer
© 2008 Inner Sanctum Studio
From the album *Raise It Up Bring It Down*

13. Jazz of Ages
(Based on "Rock of Ages" – Traditional)
Performed by Eric Komar
© 2007 Eric S. Komar (ASCAP)
From the album *Two Life*

14. Light These Lights/Chanukah Blessings
(D. Friedman)
Performed by Debbie Friedman
© 1995 Deborah Lynn Friedman
From the album *Songs of the Sprit:
    The Debbie Friedman Anthology*

Produced by Michael Boxer
    for Transcontinental Music Publications
Mastered by Stephen Fontaine
Graphic design and layout by Michael Silber